UNDERSTANDING BIBLE TEACHING

The Holy Spirit

Leon Morris MSc, M.Th, Ph.D

Scripture Union

47 Marylebone Lane, London W1 6AX

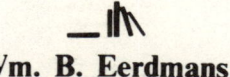

Wm. B. Eerdmans

225 Jefferson Avenue, Grand Rapids, Michigan

© 1974 Scripture Union
First published 1974
First published in this form 1978

ISBN 0 85421 713 4 (Scripture Union)
ISBN 0 8028 1769 6 (Wm. B. Eerdmans)

Printed in Great Britain at the Benham Press
by William Clowes & Sons Limited, Colchester and Beccles

General Introduction

There are many commentaries on the Biblical text and there are many systematic studies of Christian doctrine, but these studies are unique in that they comment on selected passages relating to the major teachings of the Bible. The comments are designed to bring out the doctrinal implications rather than to be a detailed verse by verse exposition, but writers have always attempted to work on the basis of sound exegetical principles. They have also aimed to write with a certain devotional warmth, and to demonstrate the contemporary relevance of the teaching.

These studies were originally designed as a daily Bible reading aid and formed part of Scripture Union's Bible Characters and Doctrines series. They can, of course, still be used in this way but experience has shown that they have a much wider use. They have a continued usefulness as a summary and exposition of Biblical teaching arranged thematically, and will serve as a guide to the major passages relating to a particular doctrine.

Writers have normally based their notes on the RSV text but readers will probably find that most modern versions are equally suitable. Many, too, have found them to be an excellent basis for group Bible study. Here the questions and themes for further study and discussion will prove particularly useful—although many individuals will also find them stimulating and refreshing.

The Holy Spirit

Leon Morris, M.Sc., M.Th., Ph.D

ONE

A Divine Person

1 : Grieving the Holy Spirit
Isaiah 63.7–14; Ephesians 4.25–32

One of the difficult things in the interpretation of the Old Testament is the extent to which the Spirit is thought of as distinct from God the Father. In the case of a man, 'the spirit' and 'the man' are not two people. The two terms are not synonymous but we cannot say that two persons are involved. What is the position with God? Clear distinctions between the Persons of the Trinity are certainly found in the New Testament but the thought that the Spirit is a Person does not seem to have been developed in Old Testament times.

The Old Testament, however, does contain passages which indicate some kind of distinction within the Godhead. Expressions like 'the angel of his presence', 'the face of the Lord', or 'the name of the Lord' point to divine activity and are best explained in terms of something other than a unitarian understanding of the nature of God. In view of the fact that devout Jewish students, who take the whole Old Testament as divinely inspired, do not see the Spirit as separate in any way from the Father, we cannot say that the distinct personality of the Spirit is a necessary deduction from the Old Testament. But we can say that passages like Isa. 63 gain in force when we understand them in the light of the fuller revelation of the New Testament.

The prophet pictures God as loving and merciful (7). He has a deep and tender concern for His people and feels for them in their affliction. He saved them and redeemed them and 'carried them all the days of old' (9). It might have been expected that they would respond to this. But they did not. They rebelled. And they 'grieved his holy Spirit' (10). Now grief is something that we ascribe to persons only. It is meaningless to speak of a thing as 'grieved'. The Spirit is thus a Person, active and concerned for the people of God—One, moreover, who is deeply involved in their reaction to the divine leading. We ought never to think that

5

God is not greatly interested in the way we react to His good gifts. His Holy Spirit is grieved when we rebel.

So it is when Paul speaks of the kind of conduct that should characterize the Christian and goes on, 'do not grieve the Holy Spirit of God' (Eph. 4.30). Right through the Bible the Spirit of God is passionately concerned that God's people live as the people of God should. He is sharply opposed to all evil and is grieved when they give way to it. Hermas, a second-century Christian writer, calls the Spirit 'a cheerful Spirit' (using the Greek adjective *hilaron*, from which we get our word 'hilarity'). We should be clear that the Spirit is not a killjoy. And that we should avoid the kind of conduct that grieves this cheerful Person.

2 : The Spirit in the Church

Haggai 2.1–9; Acts 5.1–11

Theoretically, it would be possible to think of the Spirit as simply an influence, a force at work among the people of God and others. But the language used in both Old and New Testaments is such as to exclude this. The Spirit is not spoken of impersonally but in terms we naturally use of persons. Thus Haggai pictures the people after their return from the Exile, depressed and uncertain of themselves. They had undergone hardships and were doubtless wondering whether they had done the right thing in returning to the land of their fathers. The prophet encouraged them and they built the Temple of God which had fallen into ruins. Inevitably some who remembered the glory of the former building complained about the new one. In reply Haggai points out that in a very real sense the new Temple had a greater glory than the older one. That had been built by the wealthy Solomon and represented the generosity of a king who could well afford it. This new Temple was built by a people who were poor and without resource. It meant hard work and very real sacrifice. And this the Lord honours. Haggai puts the main emphasis of his encouragement on the fact that God is with the people. God says, 'I am with you' and again, 'My Spirit abides among you' (4 f.). The word translated 'abides' (literally 'stands') can indicate a permanent stay. We would not misinterpret it here if we translated, 'My Spirit lives with you'. It is this dynamic and living

Person who brings strength and inspiration to the dispirited Jews.

The well-known story of Ananias and Sapphira points a very different moral, but it likewise stresses the dynamic presence of a living Person. When Ananias told his lie in the presence of the church's representatives Peter spoke of this as a lie not to men, but to the Holy Spirit (3). The same apostle pointed out to Sapphira that her conspiracy with her husband was in fact an agreement to test out (so rather than 'tempt') the Holy Spirit (9).

The Spirit lives among people. He can be lied to. He can be tested out. How can we understand these things other than of a Person and a great divine Person at that?

3 : The Spirit Within

1 Corinthians 2

Paul has three important things to tell us about the Spirit in this chapter. First, effective preaching of the gospel is done in the power of the Spirit (4 f.). We ought never to think that it is great preaching or great organizing that brings men to Christ. God can, and does, honour such good works of His servants. But the gospel is powerful only when the Spirit of God is in it. It is the Spirit who speaks to the hearts of men, the Spirit who brings conviction of the truth of the gospel message, the Spirit who enables men to respond in repentance and faith.

The second point is that the Spirit is, so to speak, on the 'inside' of God (11). Paul uses the illustration of a man. Nobody knows what is going on inside a man. He may appear to be interested in an activity that is going on before him, while miles away in thought. From the outside another man can guess more or less accurately at the man's inner processes, but he cannot know them. Only 'the spirit of the man which is in him' really knows. In the same way it is only the Spirit of God who knows the thoughts of God. Men, especially spiritually-minded men, may guess at the ways of God. But they can know of them only what has been revealed. The Spirit's knowledge of God is different. He knows God from the inside and thus He knows God perfectly. Even the depths of God are open to His searchings (10).

The third point is that this divine Person, who knows God

from the inside, does not keep all this knowledge to Himself. He reveals some of it to men. The Spirit is given to men and He brings understanding of God's gifts (12). He teaches men the words to use (13) and He interprets spiritual truths (13). Paul is not talking about the insight possessed by the natural or unspiritual man (14). He is talking about a God-given gift. All this can be no less than the working of a great divine Person who comes to men.

4 : The Spirit Sets Men Free

Romans 8.9–11; 2 Corinthians 3

It is of the utmost importance to be clear that the presence of the Spirit is not some optional extra to be found, so to speak, in the lives of super-Christians only. He is found in every believer and no one belongs to Christ unless the Spirit is in him (Rom. 8.9). This means more than a minor difference in non-essential matters. The Spirit's presence means radical revolution. So Paul speaks of the death of the body (Rom. 8.10), by which he probably means an end to the power of what he elsewhere calls 'the body of sin' (Rom. 6.6, cf. 6.12; 7.24; 8.13). When a man comes to Christ the lower nature no longer dominates. Instead the Spirit of God transforms the man and makes him really alive. The life the believer has, he has because of the Spirit of God within him (Rom. 8.11).

It is this basic truth which enables Paul to speak of his Corinthian friends as a letter written 'with the Spirit of the living God' (2 Cor. 3.3). The Spirit is not a minor influence, but is so dominant that their lives are a page 'written' by Him. This leads on to the thought that the whole Christian way is a way dominated by the Spirit. There is dispute as to whether Paul is specifically referring to the divine Spirit in his contrast with the letter, but none that it is the Spirit of God who gives the Christian life its peculiar power and special flavour. The presence of the Spirit transforms life and releases men from the bondage to the letter of the law that characterized the Jewish way.

There is further difficulty about 'the Lord is the Spirit' (2 Cor. 3.17). Some commentators (e.g. Tasker) think there is an explicit reference to the Holy Spirit. Others (e.g. Hughes) think it is Christ who is in mind. But none disputes that the life of which

Paul writes is a life enriched with the liberty the Spirit of God gives. 'Where the Spirit of the Lord is, there is freedom.'

Throughout today's passages, then, there runs the thought that the Holy Spirit is a Person who is concerned that men should live the fullest and freest of lives. When He comes into a man it is in order that that man be liberated and brought into the glorious experience of fellowship with God with all that that means in terms of power and liberty and joy. This cannot be less than the work of a divine Person.

5 : The Temple of God

1 Corinthians 3.16, 17; 2 Corinthians 6.14–7.1

In antiquity, temples were often built on a grand scale and they were usually richly adorned from the offerings of worshippers. Ordinary people lived in drab surroundings and the homes of the poor were shoddy. So they regarded their visits to temples as great occasions. In addition to being centres of worship, temples were places to meet people and often to transact a variety of business. But what characterized the temple above all else was that it was the home of the god. That was what gave it its special significance no matter what secular activities the worshipper might pursue there. It was his god's presence that governed his conduct when he was at the temple.

Paul has a revolutionary thought when he tells the Corinthians, not that they are in God's temple, but that they *are* that temple. Lest they miss the significance of what he is saying he underlines it: 'God's Spirit dwells in you' (1 Cor. 3.16). Just as a temple is set apart from all other buildings, so are Christians set apart from all other men (2 Cor. 6.15 f.). A temple is holy. It is to be used for no other purpose than the service of the god. The temple of the living God is no exception. Those in whom He lives must live as befits a temple. It is possible to regard the individual believer as a temple and sometimes the New Testament does this. But it is also possible to see the church, believers as a whole, as a temple, and that seems to be the case here, at least in ch. 3 (notice that 'temple' is singular while 'you' is plural).

'Do not be mismated with unbelievers' (2 Cor. 6.14) is often taken as referring to marriage. But Paul does not say this and we should see the passage as wider in application. It will have its reference to marriage. But Paul is saying that those who form God's temple must at all times behave accordingly. They will have contacts with non-believers, but they must beware of making of these such partnerships that their distinctive witness is compromised. Those in whom the Spirit lives must live as befits the presence of the Spirit whose characteristic designation is 'Holy'. So from another and a very practical angle we are reminded that we must see Him as a Person.

6 : Three Mighty Persons

Matthew 28.16–20; 1 Corinthians 12.4–6; 2 Corinthians 13.14

These three passages have in common that they all speak of God the Father, God the Son and God the Holy Spirit in such a way as to link them closely and to set them apart from everyone and everything else. We are so used to speaking of the Father, the Son and the Holy Spirit in this way that we do not stop to reflect that this is a curious procedure. We could not link anyone else in this fashion. We could not, for example, speak of the Father, the Son and the archangel Gabriel. This is not simply a matter of habit. It is incongruous to put anyone else there. No one, not even an archangel, fits. But every Christian recognizes the naturalness of putting Father, Son and Spirit together. The Father and the Son cannot be thought of other than as Persons and this implies that we should think of the Spirit in the same way. It would be very curious, to say the least, to associate two Persons and a force or influence.

The Matthean passage records our Lord's last appearance, when He gave His final command to the apostles. In it He charged them to evangelize 'all nations' in view of the fact that 'all authority' had been given to Him. Because of what He is they must proclaim Him throughout the world. But in making disciples and in baptizing them the apostles are not to think of Jesus as an isolated Being. In the act of baptizing they are to remember the place of the Father and the Spirit. Disciples are baptized in the name of the Spirit of God. From the beginning the Spirit is named upon them.

And this continues. Paul speaks of varieties of gifts and service, but of one God who gives the gifts and is the object of the service. And in the 'varieties of gifts' there is 'the same Spirit'

(1 Cor. **12.4**). As they engage in Christian service believers do not do so in their own strength. The gifts which enable them to serve are from the Spirit.

The 'grace' is familiar to us as a benediction. It speaks of the fellowship indwelt by, or created by, the Spirit. Either way it is the characteristic thing that the Spirit is there. Fellowship speaks of persons, and a fellowship that extends through the world and through the centuries speaks of a Person who is divine.

Questions and themes for study and discussion on Studies 1–6

1. Are there things in your life that grieve the Holy Spirit?
2. How may men lie to the Holy Spirit these days?
3. What are the implications for a Christian in today's world of the thought that the liberating work of the Holy Spirit is a work of God?
4. What does cleansing 'from every defilement of body and spirit' (2 Cor. **7.1**) mean for you?
5. How does the presence of the Spirit with believers everywhere help us understand His Person?

TWO

Active in the Universe

7 : Creator Spirit

Genesis 1.1, 2; Psalm 33.6–9

The Bible associated the Spirit of God with this created universe right from the very first. The precise function of the Spirit, however, is not clear. The verb translated 'was moving' is not a common one, but it occurs again in Deut. 32.11 of the eagle fluttering over its young. The traditional Jewish way of understanding the passage has been that the Spirit of God 'hovered' over the waters like a dove (sometimes there is added, 'without touching them' or the like). Calvin thought the idea was that it was the Spirit who held together the watery chaos and made it stable. Many commentators maintain that the use of a term associated with a bird's care for its young introduces a note of tenderness and concern, and this is probably right. Kidner holds that the use of the term forestalls 'any impression of Olympian detachment' we might possibly derive from the later part of the chapter. He adds, 'this aspect of intimate contact must be kept in mind throughout.'

In Psa. 33.6 there is perhaps a reference to 'Spirit' in the word translated 'breath' (*ruach*). At any rate the psalmist is referring to the same creative activity as that in Gen. 1 where we have already seen reason for recognizing an activity of the Spirit of God. The Old Testament not infrequently associates the gift of life with the Spirit (e.g. Job 33.4; Psa. 104.30; Isa. 44.3 f.; Ezek. 36.26 f.). Here the psalmist is stressing the greatness of God who performed the work of creation so effortlessly. In the face of creation the only appropriate attitude on the part of created man is that of awe (8). When we realize what the Spirit of God has done we can only stand abashed. This reinforces the truth we saw in our first series of studies, that the Spirit is a great divine Person. And it emphasizes the other truth that the Spirit is not absent from any part of creation. He was involved in it from the first and He continues to be involved in it.

8 : The Breath of God

Genesis 2.4–7; Job 32.6–10; 33.1–7

There is a connection in Hebrew (as in many languages) between 'breath' and 'spirit'. Early man could not see or weigh breath. But this invisible, intangible thing was necessary to life: when a man ceased to have breath he ceased to live. It was the same with the spirit of the man. That could not be seen or felt, but, however it was understood, it was necessary to life. So the same word was sometimes applied to the man's 'breath' as to his 'spirit'. In the Old Testament *ruach*, 'spirit' (either a man's spirit or God's) may also be translated 'breath' on occasion. Mostly, however, 'breath' renders *neshamah*, which was not normally used for 'spirit' (though cf. Job 26.4; Prov. 20.27). The two words, however, can come very close in meaning as we see from Elihu's words, 'The spirit of God has made me, and the breath of the Almighty gives me life' (Job 33.4). Here the parallelism shows that the two expressions, 'the spirit of God' and 'the breath of the Almighty', are similar in meaning. The statement underlines the activity of the Spirit in creation and in the giving of life to men. What we are we owe to the Spirit. And it shows that we must take seriously statements about 'the breath of God' when we are discussing the activity of the Spirit of God.

In Gen. 2 there is the story of how God formed man of dust from the ground 'and breathed into his nostrils the breath of life; and man became a living being' (7). It would be possible to take this to mean that God caused the inanimate carcass to breathe, and that that was what made it alive. But it is much more in accordance with the Old Testament view of life and of 'the breath of God' to see a reference to God's Spirit as putting the 'spirit' within man. It is the Spirit who gives life. Elihu seems to take up this meaning, and even advance it a little, when he says 'it is the spirit (*ruach*) in a man, the breath of the Almighty, that makes him understand' (Job 32.8). It is God's inbreathing that enables a man to have understanding. Not only is the Spirit responsible for life, but for life in its fullness.

9 : Life depends on God

Job 34.10–15; Psalm 104.24–30

To understand these two passages we must keep in mind the close connection in Hebrew between 'spirit' and 'breath'. It is as the Spirit of God gives living things breath that they live. Apart from this divine activity they must die. This is the point of Elihu's words in the Job passage. He sees God as just and as all-powerful. In the light of this he points out that if God were to take back 'his spirit' and gather 'his breath' all men would perish. 'His spirit' is not 'the Spirit of God' but the spirit in man that comes from the Spirit of God. In similar fashion the Preacher can describe death by saying 'the spirit returns to God who gave it' (Eccl. 12.7). Were it not that God is active in man man would die. There is nothing in man that gives him inherent power over life. He lives only as God sustains him.

In Psa. 104 the psalmist is writing of the wonder of creation. He sees God's wisdom in all His works and he is especially struck by what he sees in life in and on the sea. Like Elihu he thinks of all of life as dependent on God. It is only as God gives the creatures food that they get it (28). And like Elihu he thinks of these creatures as dying when God takes their breath (or their spirit, *ruach*). This means returning to the dust, which will be a reference to their original creation out of dust (Gen. 2.19). But unlike Elihu, the psalmist goes on to refer to the Spirit's creative work. Just as the withdrawal of the spirit or breath from the creature means death, so the presence of the divine Spirit means creative activity and life (30). It is important for us to be clear on the biblical view of the continuing activity of God in this universe. We should not see our world as something like a clock, which might be wound up, set going and left to run by itself. God is in His creation and without the sustaining work of His Spirit it must cease. We depend on God for the next breath we draw.

Employing Human Instruments under the Old Covenant

10 : The Skill of the Craftsman
Exodus 28.1–4; 31.1–11; 35.30–35

In recent times there has been an emphasis on the importance of secular life and scholars are writing books with titles like *The Secular Meaning of the Gospel*. This represents a reaction against a tendency on the part of some religious people to think of life as divisible into the sacred and secular. They saw things like worship and Bible study as activities where God's blessing might legitimately be sought and where the Spirit of God might be expected to be in operation. But the work of, say, a secretary or of a miner, was secular. The best that could be hoped for was that Christians in such occupations might do their work well and so make openings for the gospel.

Now we are realizing that we cannot divide life into two. All of life is God's. We serve Him just as really in our daily job as we do in our prayers, though the manner is different. Today's passages bring this truth out. The first of them makes it clear that the robes the priests were to wear as they went about the service of the tabernacle were not unimportant. The duly consecrated priests must serve God in the right way and the use of the robes God commanded was part of the right way (Exod. **28.**1–4). Our traditional thinking might lead to the idea that 'spiritual' work began when the robes were worn. But not so. Bezalel was 'called' to the work of making these robes (others than ministers need a sense of vocation). And he was equipped by being 'filled . . . with the Spirit of God' (Exod. **31.**1–3). Plainly the qualities set out in Exod. **31.**3 ff. come from this gift of the Spirit and not any natural endowment. And equally plainly the gifts given to Oholiab and the other workers show that the same Spirit enabled them to do their work (Exod. **31.**6 ff.; **35.**34 f.; **36.**1). This has important implications for every Christian as he works in his daily job.

11 : The Spirit and the Elders

Numbers 11.16, 17, 24–30

The Spirit's activity in inspiring the craftsmen to do their work well was important. Less obvious, perhaps, but more important was the way the Spirit enabled men to take their part in the administration and government of the people. Moses occupied a peculiar position. He was not exactly a king and it would be difficult to say exactly how far his authority extended. But the people certainly looked to him for leadership in a wide range of their activities. Quite early he had trouble getting through his many duties and his father-in-law advised him to delegate responsibility (Exod. **18**.13 ff.). But, though Moses heeded the advice and appointed subordinate officials (Exod. **18**.24 ff.), he could still be in trouble and even complain to God about his hard lot (Num. **11**.11–15).

We may perhaps feel that the Lord's servant should not have allowed himself to become irritated, even though we admit that he had good cause for his irritation. But God did not blame him. Instead, in His compassion, He made provision for the help that His servant needed so much. He told Moses to gather seventy elders who would share the responsibility and He promised that He would 'put . . . upon them' some of the same spirit that Moses had. Both in the promise and in the performance (17, 25) the RSV has 'spirit' rather than 'Spirit', a choice which can be defended. But when they received this gift the men prophesied (25), which makes it clear the gift must be thought of as a manifestation of the Spirit of God. It is important for us to see that good administration is another facet of life in which God is interested, interested enough, indeed, to put His Spirit on seventy men so that they could perform this function adequately. We must be on our guard against a sharp differentiation between 'spiritual' ministries, when prayer and preaching are prominent and 'secular' ministries, when administration and the like are in mind. Here, too, we need the Spirit. And the Spirit cannot be contained. Joshua was jealous for Moses and thought Eldad and Medad should be restrained. But the Spirit of God gives His gifts with a lavish hand. There is no way of limiting them to a few people, and we should not try. Moses shows us the more excellent way (29).

12 : The Strength of Samson

Judges 13.24–14.20

After the two previous studies which showed that the skill of the craftsman and the excellence of the administrator may come from God it is no surprise to learn that the strength of the strong has, at least on occasion, been the result of an activity of the Spirit of God. In popular treatments of Samson far too much attention has been given to the hair of the strong man and not enough to what the Bible actually says. Three times in today's passage we are reminded that it was the Spirit of the Lord who moved him and enabled him to do what he did (**13.25; 14.**6, 19, cf. **15.**14). Samson was strong, not because he had long hair, but because he was the instrument of God to effect certain purposes. In the discharge of the tasks for which he was destined from the womb (**13.**3 ff.) strength was needed, and accordingly the Spirit gave him strength.

But we should notice two things about the Spirit's gift. One is that it was intermittent. The Spirit came upon Samson at different times, apparently to give him power for individual actions. The gift given to Christians differs in that the Spirit is a continuing endowment.

The other is that Samson was, in many ways, a curious recipient of God's good gift. In the incident in today's passage he does not appear in a very good light. We see him casually picking out a Philistine girl for his wife, defiling his Nazirite consecration by handling the carcass of a dead lion (cf. Num. **6.**6), entering a wager with thirty young Philistine men, and finding himself quite unable to resist the blandishments of his bride when she tried to worm his secret out of him. It is scarcely the record we expect from a man of God. Yet God did not withdraw His Spirit from Samson at this time; and even when He did, it was not permanent (cf. **16.**20, 28 ff.). We should not conclude that the way we live does not matter. It matters very much that we live up to all that is involved in our call to be the servants of God in our day and age. But the incident shows us that God does not desert His servants when they fail. He still works out His purposes. He still sends His Spirit to them.

13 : The Spirit and the spirits

1 Samuel 16

There are only two references to the Spirit of the Lord in this chapter, those which speak of His coming on David and of His leaving Saul (13, 14). But, though this is not said explicitly, clearly it was the Spirit who enabled Samuel to see David as God's choice. The Spirit then guided Samuel to David, came on David for future service and left Saul who had departed from the ways of God.

Samuel was impressed with Eliab and was quite ready to greet him as the Lord's anointed. But the man on whom the Spirit comes is not necessarily the man that men would choose. Eliab was Samuel's choice, but he was not God's. When David was marked out by the voice giving divine approval and by the anointing which Samuel administered, the Spirit of the Lord came mightily upon him. What this means is not explained. We must take it in connection with the anointing to be king, which means that in some way the Spirit of the Lord was preparing David from that day forward for the service he was to render.

In sharp contrast is the statement that 'the Spirit of the Lord departed from Saul' (14). This man had departed so far from the ways of the Lord that the Spirit no longer equipped him for his work as king. In our last study we saw that God does not withdraw His Spirit from us when our well-intentioned efforts go astray and we slip into sin. But persistence in opposition to the ways of God is incompatible with the presence of the Spirit of God. In the last resort a man must choose to go God's way or his own. Saul chose his own way and the Spirit departed from him. We should probably connect with this the coming of the 'evil spirit from the Lord' that tormented him (14). The sacred writer sees the hand of God in everything and thus even the coming of this evil spirit had its place in the plan of God. It does not mean that God refused to help Saul and deliberately tormented him. But when Saul chose self instead of God, then in this moral order that God has set up he invited a spirit of evil to come to him. And it did. Our moral choices have far-reaching consequences.

14 : Denouncing Evil

Micah 3.5–12

Knowing when the Spirit of God was speaking through a man who claimed to be a prophet must have been a continuing problem to the men of old Israel. They heard prophets like Isaiah or Amos sounding out their 'Thus says the Lord' and recognized a word from God. They did not pay prophets a salary but there can be no doubt that they showed appreciation of what they owed to these men of God by material gifts of some kind. But then others appeared who also said, 'Thus says the Lord', e.g. Zedekiah, the son of Chenaanah (1 Kings 22.11). Such men had no word from the Lord, but how was the ordinary man to know this? And, of course, unless they recognized them as false prophets people would make the same gifts to such men as they made to the prophets of God. With such prospects before them the false prophets were irresistibly tempted to claim inspiration, and to produce 'prophecies' that would please those who asked (and paid!) for them.

It is this situation that Micah is facing. He denounces men who have led people astray with their prophecies; prophecies that were adapted to the gifts made to those uttering them (5). Micah is able to assure such men that they will lack vision and be disgraced (6 f.). How can he be so sure of this? Because the Spirit of the Lord has filled him with power to denounce sin (8). This is a tremendous advance on most of what we have seen in our earlier studies. With no intention of depreciating gifts like those of the craftsman or the strong man Samson, we can nevertheless say that ethical perception is much more important. And Micah is assuring us that his knowledge of this evil is not something that he knows out of his own resources. He knows it only because of the divine infilling. There was a constant idea in antiquity that holiness and righteousness did not necessarily go together. Men could be devoted to their god without becoming better men and this attitude spilled over into Israel. But when a man is filled with the Spirit of the Lord he has the insight to recognize this for the evil thing it is and to denounce it. The Spirit is concerned that men live uprightly. And if we have the Spirit of God we will be concerned, too.

Questions and themes for study and discussion on Studies 7-14

1. What difference does the thought of the Spirit's 'intimate contact' (Kidner) make to our understanding of Genesis 1?
2. In what areas may we expect 'the breath of the Almighty' to give us understanding?
3. What does it mean for daily living that we depend on God for our very breath?
4. What are the implications for the modern Christian of Bezalel's being 'called' to work as a craftsman?
5. How far can we agree with the hymn writer who addresses the Spirit in the words,

> *'I hate the sins that made Thee mourn
> And drove Thee from my breast'*?

6. Why is the Spirit characteristically called 'Holy'?

THREE

Preparing for the Messiah's Advent

15 : The Spirit of Wisdom
Isaiah 11.1–9

The idea of anointing is important throughout the Old Testament. It marked certain men out for special service, e.g. the king ('the Lord's anointed') or the priest ('the anointed priest'). But as the men of the Old Testament saw the inadequacies of the best of God's servants, and as they contemplated the greatness of the task men of God should be doing, they were led by the Holy Spirit to look for the coming in due time of One who would be specially important in God's working out of His will. This One would be not 'an' anointed, but 'the' anointed, or, to use the technical term, the Messiah. This is our transliteration of the Hebrew word meaning 'anointed' (translated into Greek it becomes *Christos* from which we get 'Christ'). The term itself does not often occur, but the idea is widespread in the Old Testament.

In today's passage we learn that the Messiah will be a descendant of Jesse (David's father; i.e. he would be of Davidic stock). Immediately, the prophet goes on to the thought that the Spirit of the Lord will 'rest upon him'. The Spirit came upon Jesus as He commenced His mission (Mark 1.10). While there are not many references to the Spirit during the ministry of our Lord, the general impression the Gospels leave is that the Spirit rested upon Him throughout His earthly life, as later studies will show. In other words we see in the Gospels the fulfilment of what is here foreshadowed. The Spirit was the essential equipment of the Messiah.

Included among the gifts that the Spirit will bring are 'wisdom', 'understanding', 'counsel' and 'knowledge'. While distinct these are clearly related and they indicate the importance of *ideas* in Messiah's work. Earthly power is not important, as we see from Jesus' ministry. He never accepted the current view that the Messiah would win a military triumph over the Romans. Yet the Spirit did give Him 'might', power in the spiritual realm which we may not unfairly connect with 'the fear of the Lord', which ensured the completion of the programme envisaged in today's passage. Nobody can resist Him as He implements the heavenly wisdom. The Spirit of the Lord sees to it that the true wisdom and not some merely earthly knowledge is at work in the messianic programme. In the modern confusion this still bears thinking about.

16 : The Servant of the Lord

Isaiah 42.1–4; 61.1–4

The Servant of the Lord is a great figure in certain poems in the latter part of the prophecy of Isaiah. When we read these, especially Isa. **52.13–53.12**, we are usually taken up with the way in which they set forth the atoning ministry of our Lord. This must always be of absorbing interest to God's people, but it is worth noticing also that there are passages, like those now before us, which bring out the place of the Spirit in the work of the Servant. As we saw in our last study, the Spirit came on Jesus as He began His ministry. Now we see something of what that means.

In the first passage the emphasis is on the discouraged and the defeated, the 'bruised reed' and the 'dimly burning wick'. In ancient Palestine reeds and wicks were cheap and plentiful. For most people it was not worth persisting with a defective example of either. Simpler by far to throw it away and start again. But the Spirit-filled Servant of the Lord does not do this with damaged lives. He does not act as the world does, He saves them and persists to final victory. And this is right. It means justice as well as mercy (**42.1, 4**). There is guidance here for the servants of the Lord as they engage in their lesser ministries.

There is a peculiar interest in Isa. **61**, for Jesus Himself chose to use these words when He spoke about His own ministry. After reading the opening part of our passage in the synagogue at Nazareth, He said to the people, 'Today this scripture has been fulfilled in your hearing' (Luke **4**.21). The reference to anointing (**61**.1) seems to show that what follows is the messianic task: our Lord's use of the passage makes this sure. The Spirit anointed Him for the work that He was to do throughout His ministry. The 'good tidings' Jesus preached was not a message of human origin, but one due to the Spirit's anointing. Right through the passage there runs a deep concern for the afflicted. The gospel is not a message for the comfortable, but for those in trouble. For such the Spirit-filled Messiah has a message. His saving work makes good 'the devastations of many generations' (**61.4**).

17 : The Transforming Spirit

Isaiah 32.9–20; 43.25–44.5

In both today's passages there is a contrast between the tragic consequences of sin and the vigorous life the Spirit of God gives. Consistently the Old Testament teaches that when men sin punishment follows. It is not always immediate, but it is sure. The truth is illustrated over and over again in the history of the chosen people. In accordance with this Isa. **32.**9–14 has a striking picture of complacent Israel and of the inevitable consequence of Israel's sin. In this case the disaster is forecast in little more than a year (**10**). God's punishment will be seen in the failure of the agricultural processes (**10**) with the consequent desolation of both city and countryside (**14**). Later the prophet speaks of God's punishment of the evil of other nations (**43.14**). We should be clear that, while men may sin for a time with impunity, in the end sin always pays its wages.

But the emphasis in both our passages is not on sin and its ill deserts, but on God's good gift in sending the Spirit. When the Spirit is poured out there will be effects in nature (**32.15**), but even more in moral qualities—justice, righteousness, peace, quietness and trust. In days like our own there is need for stress, first on the fact that these things come as the result of God's good gift, not man's endeavour, and secondly that it is not peace that comes first but justice and righteousness. Peace is the effect of righteousness (**32.17**), not a good that can be obtained quite apart from righteousness.

Though all this was held out to the Israelites of old, in fact, the prophet saw that the men of his day would not yield to the Spirit and find the blessing. So he spoke of Him as coming on their descendants (**44.3**). We notice two things of importance. First, God does not go back on His purpose or His promise. The word is expressly addressed to Jacob and to Israel (**44.**1). Secondly, the full outpouring of the blessing awaited the coming of the Messiah. It was only as the result of His saving work that men received the Spirit in His fullness.

18 : The Vindication of God

Ezekiel 36.22–38; 39.25–29

The Exile was one of the great pivotal events of Israelite history. The Old Testament leaves us in no doubt about the shattering effect it had on the nation. Before it some had thought comfortably that in the last resort God must intervene to save His people, as He had done when Sennacherib threatened (2 Kings 19.35 f.). After it they knew that God viewed sin as so serious that He was quite capable of allowing their enemies to triumph over them when they sinned.

Today we are concerned with the vindication of God in the transformation of His people. The prophet points out that, in what had happened, God's name was profaned among the nations (36.23). This would not be allowed to continue. God would bring His people home. But He is a moral God and He would not bring them back simply in order that they might resume their old sinful practices. So He speaks of cleansing them from their idolatry (36.25). The worst thing about the people, however, was not their outward worshipping of idols but their inward state of heart and spirit. So God says that He will give them 'a new heart' and put 'a new spirit' in them (36.26). This might be taken to mean that God would enable them to look at life in a different spirit. But the word from God proceeds, 'I will put my spirit within you' (36.27), and this should surely be taken to mean 'the Spirit of God'. It was necessary that the people make a clean break with sin and that they live lives honouring to God. But they had showed over and over again that they were quite unable to do this. They needed a strength not their own. What God now says to them is that that strength will be given them. His own Spirit will come into them and He will enable them to live as they never could have lived left to themselves. They will be able to observe God's commandments (36.27) and turn from evil (36.31). Our second passage carries the same basic message and it culminates in the promise of the pouring out of God's Spirit (39.29).

There is a sense, of course, in which all this took place at the return from the Exile. But the fulfilment then was at best partial. Really to put away sin was the work of the Lord Jesus, and the fullness of the Spirit's indwelling was the fruit of His work.

19 : The Spirit and All Flesh

Joel 2.15–32

The call to repentance (15–17) is followed by the announcement of the Lord's blessing (18–27). The sequence is important. The blessing of God is not a gift given without regard to ethical and moral considerations. A dallying with sin and the indwelling of the Spirit do not go together, which perhaps explains some of the powerlessness in the modern Church. But when sin is grieved over and put away the way is prepared for the coming of God's Spirit. Joel speaks of all manner of blessings as he leads up to the Spirit. But repentance is the prerequisite of them all.

He looks for the coming of the Spirit at some future time ('afterward', v. 28). God says that He will pour out the Spirit 'on all flesh'. This does not mean on every member of the human race without distinction, but it does mean that the Spirit will not be restricted to a select few. In our earlier studies we have seen how the Spirit came upon outstanding individuals and equipped them for unusual work. But in the time of which Joel speaks all God's people will receive the Spirit. He goes on to the results. 'Your sons and your daughters shall prophesy' removes any distinction of sex. There is similarly no distinction between old and young. We should probably not put a difference between dreaming dreams and seeing visions. Poetic parallelism makes these much the same and neither differs greatly from prophesying. All are ways in which God reveals His will. It is most interesting that 'the menservants and maidservants' (i.e. slaves) are included among those receiving the Spirit, for, in antiquity, most people would not have seen these lowly folk as suitable recipients of God's great gift. But God's Spirit is for all God's people without distinction.

We should not take the 'blood and fire and columns of smoke' literally, for Peter claimed the fulfilment of this prophecy at the day of Pentecost (Acts 2.16–21). They are part of the picture. Verses 30–32 make it clear that the outpouring of the Spirit spoken of ushers in the messianic age. The work of Messiah and the gift of the Spirit go hand in hand.

20: The Forerunner

Luke 1.13–17, 39–45

We have seen that in Old Testament days the Spirit did many things in preparation for the coming of the Messiah. It is not surprising accordingly to find Him at work in John the Baptist, who was to be the immediate forerunner of the Lord. John's birth was unusual in that both his parents were 'advanced in years' (Luke 1.7). But not only was his conception unusual, the child was to have an unusual gift of the Spirit right from the womb (15). Following on this we are told of his special task. This is described in various ways and summed up in the words, 'to make ready for the Lord a people prepared' (17). The clear implication is that the preparation of a people for the Messiah was a task that needed the special equipment of the Holy Spirit. It could not be done on the merely human level. The interesting thing is that while the Spirit was to fill John the Baptist the emphasis is not on that great prophet, but on Messiah who would come.

It is the same with our second passage. Elizabeth was filled with the Spirit when she met Mary. As a result she uttered a little poem (it is printed as prose in the RSV, but it is really poetry). In it she does not exult in the son who is to be born of her, as might have been expected. In fact she does not mention him except as he leaped in her womb to greet his Lord. It is Mary's son on whom the Spirit-filled Elizabeth concentrates. So she pronounces Mary blessed, clearly because of the Son she was to bear. She goes on to speak of Him as 'my Lord' and to interpret (under the Spirit's leading) the movement of the babe in her own womb as a leaping for joy at the approach of the mother of the Lord. We see the same thing in the song of Zechariah (Luke 1.68–79), a song uttered when the old priest was filled with the Holy Spirit. His first words after receiving back his speech were not a celebration of his personal relief, nor a thanksgiving for his own small son, but a thanksgiving for God's sending His Messiah. The Spirit centres on the divine action for all mankind.

21 : The Glory and the Gloom

Luke 2.22–35

Simeon comes before us only in this incident. He is usually thought of as an old man, but Luke does not say this. He was both righteous (i.e. he did his duty towards men) and devout (and that towards God). But what distinguished him from other people was that 'the Holy Spirit was upon him' (25).

It was the continuing presence of the Spirit with him that made him so outstanding. As we have seen, under the old dispensation the Holy Spirit came on people for special occasions, but a continuous presence of the Spirit was rare. Clearly Simeon was an unusual man, and one who lived very close to God.

One specific revelation the Spirit had made to him was that he would see the Christ of God before he died. Thus his presence in the Temple when Joseph and Mary came to make the prescribed offerings (Exod. 13.2, 12, 15; Lev. 12.1–8; Num. 18.15 f.) was not accidental. It was God's providential way of accomplishing the fulfilment of His promise. Simeon celebrated the occasion with a little song which has been greatly loved and greatly used by generations of Christian worshippers. In it he refers to God's 'salvation' by which he means the Child through whom, in due course, God's salvation would be accomplished. This would have its effects on both Gentiles and Jews. The link of revelation with Gentiles and glory with Israel should not be pressed. Both gifts will come to both groups though there is special fitness in linking glory with Israel in view of the importance of the concept in the Old Testament.

Simeon went on to notice something of what this would mean. The 'fall and rising' may mean that people must become humble before they can be exalted, or it may point to a division on account of Christ, those who accept Him being raised, while those who reject Him fall. This salvation will not be purchased without cost. The Spirit-inspired Simeon goes on to refer to the 'sword' that will pierce Mary's soul. The imagery is vivid. The cross will mean suffering for Mary as well as for Jesus. This prophecy, with Jesus still a baby, underlines the purpose worked out in the cross. That was the way God had always planned to save men. But it needed the inspiration of the Spirit for this to be seen.

22 : John's Witness to the Spirit

John 1.19–34

Only one thing is recorded about John the Baptist in the Fourth Gospel; he bore witness to Jesus. The increasing curtness of his answers to the questions in the first part of our passage is connected with this. He wanted to bear witness to Jesus and these people kept asking him questions about himself. But he did manage to do what he aimed at and pointed men to the greater than he, whose sandal he was not worthy to untie (26 f.).

He speaks of Him as 'the Lamb of God' and then goes on to bear further witness. He saw the Spirit come down from heaven like a dove (32). The reason for this imagery is not known. The dove was not, as is often said, a symbol for the Spirit (it became so among the Christians as a result of reflection on this passage and the parallels; but it is not found previously). It was sometimes used for Israel and perhaps we are to think of the reception of the Spirit as marking Jesus out as the true Israelite. And not only did the Spirit come down on Jesus, but He 'remained on him' (32), a detail not in the other Gospels. This points to a permanent endowment.

When John goes on to say that he did not know Him, it is uncertain whether he means that he did not know Jesus at all (which is possible; although related to Him, he had been brought up in the wilderness, Luke 1.80), or that he did not know that He was the Messiah. Either way, it was the descent of the Spirit that brought conviction. He had been given a sign and knew that the One on whom the Spirit came was the Messiah. Again we see the importance of the Spirit for Messiahship.

And we see something further, for John goes on to say that the revelation made to him included the information that Messiah is 'he who baptizes with the Holy Spirit' (33). It is through Jesus that men are brought into vital contact with the Spirit of God. The figure of baptism stresses abundant supply. The Spirit is given with no grudging hand. There is a quality of life that Christ makes available for men and which is characterized by the continuing presence of the Spirit of the living God.

Questions and themes for study and discussion on Studies 15-22

1. What do you see as the importance of the gifts of Isa. 11.2 in the light of the present day?

2. What relevance has the Spirit's concern for justice (Isa. 42.1, 4) to your situation?
3. How far can we apply the words of Isa. 32.17 to the modern world situation?
4. What is the importance of the gift of the Spirit to slaves?
5. John the Baptist's task required him to be filled with the Spirit. Do you see this as the general rule?
6. Reflect on the importance of John's emphasis on the fact that the Messiah would baptize with the Holy Spirit.

FOUR

The Spirit and the Lord Jesus

23 : Holy Child, Son of God

Luke 1.26–38

We have seen that the Holy Spirit was active in a variety of ways in preparing men for the coming of the Messiah. It is not at all surprising, accordingly, to find Him at work in the process whereby the Messiah was born. The angel Gabriel spoke of the One who was to be born in terms which make it clear that He was to be the Messiah (vs. 32 f.), as well as indicating something of the nature of His work for men by telling Mary that His name was to be 'Jesus' ('Saviour'). Mary's question (34) is a little puzzling, since she was engaged and must have expected to have children after marriage. Evidently she took the angel's words to mean that she would become pregnant without further intervention, perhaps immediately.

Gabriel's answer comes with delicate reticence (35). Here is a divine action described with reverent reserve. In this it is essentially different from the heathen stories sometimes adduced as parallels. They are stories of lust, of a god mating with a woman. This is a story of a virginal conception, an event in a very different category. The action of the Holy Spirit is essential to the whole process. The Child who is to be born will be called 'holy' and 'Son of God'. But this will be, Gabriel says, because of what the Spirit does. We generally think only of the second Person of the Trinity when we think of the Incarnation, with perhaps a glance at the Father. But Gabriel makes it clear that the Spirit is not only concerned, but that He actively initiates the process. Clearly all three Persons are involved in one way or another.

The final section of today's passage encourages Mary with the thought that what had happened to Elizabeth showed what God can do. Where the Holy Spirit is at work nothing is impossible (37). And Mary goes on to accept what the Spirit would do in her (38). It is important that we be found co-operating with the Spirit in His great work in men and not stubbornly opposing. It is the way of acceptance that leads to blessing, whatever hazards lie on the way.

24 : Beginning with the Spirit

Luke 3.21, 22; 4.1–21

Clearly the baptism of Jesus by John was a very impressive and important occasion. It marked the identification of Jesus with sinful men whom He had come to save. And as He thus was set apart for the mission on which God sent Him, He received the gift of the Holy Spirit as His equipment. Luke alone tells us that the Spirit came, not at the baptism itself, but just afterwards as Jesus was praying. If the Messiah was to do His God-given work He must have the Spirit. And the Spirit was given.

But the question remained: What kind of Messiah was Jesus to be? The Spirit was concerned in the time of testing that sorted this out. Matthew and Mark tell us that it was the Spirit who brought Jesus into the wilderness, but only Luke that Jesus was 'full of the Holy Spirit' at that time. He goes on to say that Jesus was led 'in the Spirit' (not 'by' as the RSV). It is too much to say that the temptation that followed was due to the Spirit. It was due to Satan. But we can say that the Spirit was there to over-rule Satan so that the ultimate result of the temptation was good and not evil, and there was therefore a Divine purpose in it. As Jesus resisted the evil one it became clear that in His ministry He would not be concerned with making bread or with establishing a worldly empire or with working spectacular but pointless miracles.

After the temptation it was 'in the power of the Spirit' that Jesus returned to Galilee and began His ministry (4.14 f.). Again we are to discern the importance of the presence of the Spirit if a ministry is to be in accordance with the mind of God. Jesus did not go about His preaching in isolation, so to speak, but only as the Spirit was with Him.

And in the synagogue at Nazareth He made it clear that He would do His characteristic work only as the Spirit directed. He read in the synagogue service the words of Isa. 61.1 f. with a phrase from 58.6. These words express the truth that when the Spirit of the Lord comes upon the Servant of the Lord a ministry to the poor, the captives, the blind and the oppressed follows.

The ministry of Jesus to the outcasts was under the inspiration of the Spirit.

25 : The Ultimate Blasphemy

Luke 11.9–13; 12.8–12

God has no favourites. If one man gives every evidence of the presence of the Holy Spirit in his life and another no sign at all, then this is not because God is more than kind to the former and more than harsh to the latter. The difference is in the men themselves. For God's good gifts, while open to all, must be sought. Asking is the first step and if we do not ask we must not expect to receive. But the genuine seeker finds (**11.9 f.**). Jesus makes the point that when even men, who are basically evil, give good gifts to their children we must see that God, who is all goodness, will give the best, the Holy Spirit, to those who ask (**11.13**). This does not mean that every casual request for the Spirit will be granted. But it does mean that no genuine seeker is refused.

The availability of this gift puts a heavy responsibility on men. Not to make use of the opportunity is a serious matter. It is in this light that we should understand the second of today's passages. The blasphemy against the Holy Spirit of which Jesus speaks (**12.10**) and for which there is no forgiveness is not a matter of words only. No form of words can ever be so serious that there is no forgiveness. But blasphemy can be a matter of attitude and action as well as of speech—the expression of a total life-style. Matthew and Mark both tell us that Jesus uttered these words as part of His response to the accusation that He cast out devils by Beelzebul (Matt. **12.24–32**; Mark **3.22–30**). To call good evil is to line up with the evil one himself. It is to deny one's best insights. It is 'the lie in the soul'. This attitude is a rejection of the Spirit's leading, a turning away from God's direction of the life, and it is this that is the ultimate blasphemy. When a man sets himself against God in this way he cuts himself off from the possibility of forgiveness. No mere words can do this—but the whole attitude of the life can.

But Jesus' teaching about the Holy Spirit is not negative. It is true that to blaspheme the Spirit is the most serious of sins and thus He gives us a solemn warning. But He goes on immediately to the thought that the Spirit gives those who accept His gracious invitation all the help they need. Even when they are in the worst troubles the world can devise and stand before 'the rulers and the authorities' (12.11) they need not be anxious. The Spirit will guide them. And if His help is adequate even for such crises how much more in the ordinary affairs of everyday life!

26 : Anointed with the Holy Spirit

Acts 10.34–43

We have seen how the Holy Spirit was active in the long years of preparation that led up to the coming of the Messiah, and in our recent readings we have been reminded of the way the Spirit was present at the beginning of our Lord's ministry and at some points within it. Now we see in Peter's speech that the Spirit was active throughout. There is still the thought of the Spirit's work in preparation, for the apostle speaks of all the prophets as bearing their witness to Jesus, and specifically to the fact that forgiveness of sins would take place through His name (43). They could do this only as the Spirit inspired them. But the emphasis is rather on the anointing that enabled Jesus to do good and to heal (38). We are aware that if we are to have any success as we seek to live for God we must have the help of the Spirit, but we do not often reflect that in this, as in so much else, Jesus is our example. He was completely responsive to the leading of the Spirit and thus He accomplished His work of goodness and of healing.

Peter speaks specifically of healing 'all that were oppressed by the devil'. In part this will refer to healing of physical illness (cf. Luke 13.16). We cannot say that all illness is directly caused by the evil one, but some is. Satan's works, moreover, do not stop on the physical level. He afflicts people in many ways. In the power of the Spirit Jesus delivered them. Peter goes on to remind his hearers that this was not a painless process. It meant the death of the Son of God (39). The anointing of the Spirit is never a guarantee that life will be easy. It means simply that God's will will be done, and that is the really important thing. And as the passion and death of Jesus were followed by His triumphant resurrection, so His followers can look for the Spirit to lead them through whatever suffering and difficulties their service of God entails into the triumph God has for His own.

Questions and themes for study and discussion on Studies 23-26

1. What values for Christian faith do you see in the virgin conception of Christ?
2. What implications do you see for your own service of God in the presence of the Spirit at the opening of Jesus' ministry?
3. 'If a man fears he may have committed the unforgivable sin that in itself is evidence that he has not.' Why is this so?
4. What difference does the anointing with the Holy Spirit and with power mean to you?

FIVE

His Coming at Pentecost

27 : The Paraclete

John 14.15–18, 25–27

On the last night before the crucifixion Jesus prophesied the coming of the Holy Spirit. He spoke of Him as the *parakletos,* which RSV translates as 'Counsellor'. This preserves the legal flavour of the original, for the Greek term often has a legal application. This leads many to suggest a rendering like 'Advocate'. What such terms do not bring out is the fact that the term is not specific. Anyone who spoke up for the accused at his trial was a *parakletos,* and not only the legal man who looked after the case for the defence. No one English word is an adequate equivalent, which is doubtless why so often we simply transliterate with Paraclete. And some of this Paraclete's functions are not legal at all. Thus He is to be with believers for ever (16) and to teach and remind them of Jesus' teaching (26). The word points to the Spirit as our Friend, especially our Friend at court.

In a sense He takes the place of Jesus, for He is with believers after Jesus' departure from the earth (16 f.). In this capacity He sees to it that Jesus' teaching is not forgotten (26). But there are other things. He is 'the Spirit of truth' (17), an unusual expression, but found also in the Dead Sea Scrolls and in the Jewish *Testament of Judah.* In neither place however does it have a content like that here. Jesus speaks of the Spirit as specially interested in truth (as is the Father, John 4.23 f., and the Son, John 14.6). Probably the expression means that He communicates the truth.

We should also notice that the Spirit is called 'the Holy Spirit' (26). It is important that the Spirit's characteristic designation is not concerned with power or majesty or knowledge or the like. It emphasizes holiness. We should not miss the implication for our own lives. It is easy to be concerned primarily with absorbing questions of doctrine or prophecy or 'secular Christianity' while we sit loose to God's demand that we be His holy servants in the world and to His provision of the Holy Spirit to enable us to be so. First of all, and above all, the Spirit is the Holy Spirit.

28 : Convincing the World

John 15.18–16.15

The Church has given a good deal of attention to the statement that the Spirit 'proceeds from the Father' (**15.**26) and has concluded that, whereas the Son is 'begotten' of the Father, the Spirit 'proceeds' (both terms refer in the Creeds to the *eternal* relationship of the Persons). This, however, while sound doctrine, does not arise from this passage. The meaning rather is that the Spirit comes from the Father to continue on earth the work of the Son. He witnesses to the Son (**15.**26), He is sent by Him (**15.**26; **16.**7), He will glorify Him and 'take what is' His 'and declare it' (**16.**14 f.). This vital presence is for the good of the Church. It has never been easy for Christians to realize that it is better for them to have the Spirit among them than the visible Jesus, but our Lord assures us that this is so (**16.**7).

The Spirit's work of convincing the world (**16.**8 ff.) is clearly important, but it is not easy to understand. It is the one work which the New Testament tells us the Spirit does in the world (elsewhere He works among believers). The RSV's 'convince' is probably better 'convict'. It means to bring home the guilt. The Spirit acts as Prosecutor and shows that the world is guilty. He also brings this home to the world itself (cf. TEV, 'he will prove to the people of the world that they are wrong about sin . . .'). Only the Spirit can convict a worldly man of his sin. Verse 9 may mean that the world has wrong ideas of sin as is shown in its unbelief, that its unbelief illustrates its sin, or that its unbelief is its sin. Perhaps all three meanings are present. The righteousness shown by Jesus' going to the Father must be the righteousness established by the cross, and it is there, too, that Satan is judged (cf. **12.**31). But none of this is apparent to the natural man. It requires a work of the Holy Spirit for him to see it.

The Spirit's ongoing work guides the people of God 'into all the truth' (**16.**13). There are, of course, no finally authoritative writings for the Christian after the New Testament, but the Spirit continually unfolds the meaning of what Christ has said and done.

29 : Jesus and the Spirit

John 7.37–39; 20.19–23

Both these important passages connect the gift of the Spirit with the Lord Jesus. The first assures us that the gift depends on Jesus' death for men, His being 'glorified' (7.39). In John's Gospel the concept of glory is linked paradoxically with lowliness. True glory is seen not in outward splendour but in humble service, and particularly in the death on the cross. There is no Greek word corresponding to 'given'. The text says, 'it was not yet Spirit'. The Spirit was not inactive in Old Testament times nor in the period covered by the Gospels. But there was nothing in either to compare with what happened on and after the day of Pentecost. That day ushered in the era of the Spirit. Then 'it was Spirit' as it had never been previously. Jesus is teaching that Calvary was necessary before the Pentecostal outpouring. The work of the Son is the necessary foundation for that of the Spirit. Notice further that 'living water' refers to the Spirit. This enables us to interpret passages like John 4 which speak of 'living water' but do not explain it.

There has been endless controversy about our second passage. Whatever view we accept there are difficulties. It seems best to understand it along the lines of Paul's words, 'there are varieties of gifts, but the same Spirit' (1 Cor. 12.4). This is not another account of the happenings of Acts 2 but something quite different. Jesus here sends His followers into the world: 'As the Father has sent me, even so I send you' (20.21). Then He equips them for this mission. He breathed and said, 'Receive the Holy Spirit' (20.22). There is no 'on them' in the Greek: the gift is to the Church as such, not its individual members. This Spirit-filled Church can proclaim the forgiveness of sins. Some take these words to refer to a power given to an individual priest to grant absolution. But the word 'any' is plural both times. Jesus is referring to groups or classes, not individuals. It is also relevant that He is speaking to disciples (20.19) not the apostles (and thus not to the 'ministry'). The gathering is surely that mentioned in Luke 24.33 ff. which included Cleopas and his companion. Jesus is giving the Spirit-filled Church the power to proclaim authoritatively the forgiveness of sins and the certainty of judgement on those who do not seek forgiveness.

30 : The Promise and the Power

Luke 24.44–53; Acts 1.1–14

In both these passages Luke tells us of some of the things the risen Lord taught the disciples as He pointed them forward to the coming of the Holy Spirit. We notice particularly the stress on the promise and the power. In both passages Jesus reminds the disciples of God's promise (Luke **24**.49; Acts **1**.4). Indeed, in the first of them Jesus calls the Spirit the promise: 'behold, I send the promise of my Father upon you'. This unusual way of speaking stresses the fact that the Spirit is not a possession that men win by their own efforts or saintliness. He is given as God's free gift, in accordance with God's free promise.

Jesus further told the disciples to 'stay in the city' (Luke **24**.49; Acts **1**.4). He did not say why there should be this period of waiting, but made it clear that they should wait. It is often easier to engage in some vigorous activity than to wait quietly. But it is fatal to try to engage in Christian service in our own unaided strength. Whatever waiting is necessary must be accepted.

For in due course, Jesus said, God would send the power. He spoke of their being 'clothed with power' (Luke **24**.49), and of their receiving power when the Holy Spirit came on them (Acts **1**.8). If there is a time for waiting there is also a time for acting. When the Spirit came upon them the disciples would be busy, and busy in an effective and purposeful way. There is a pronounced contrast between the disciples before the Spirit came and after that event. Before, they hid themselves out of the way behind locked doors (John **20**.19). Afterwards, they were different men. They made their mistakes, of course, but there is no record of their ever being afraid again. Their whole manner of life was changed when the power of God came upon them. There is more to the coming of the Spirit than power, but this is an important factor.

31 : The Coming of the Spirit

Acts 2.1–21, 36–42

The decisive empowering of the Christian Church by the Holy Spirit of God took place on the day of Pentecost following Jesus' ascension. As we have seen in recent studies the work of

Christ was the necessary precondition of the coming of the Spirit in His fullness. First Jesus must die and rise, and only after that would the Spirit be given to His followers. But now the time had come.

There were physical phenomena. The disciples heard something that sounded like 'the rush of a mighty wind'. This sound filled all the house. They also saw something. It looked like flames of fire which came and rested on each of them. But the really important thing was not anything outward. It was inward: 'they were all filled with the Holy Spirit' (4). The divine presence now filled their hearts and from this time on they were never without the Spirit of God within them. Day by day they had access to the infinite resources of God Himself. That meant new power for living and new direction for life.

As the Spirit came upon them they 'began to speak in other tongues, as the Spirit gave them utterance' (4). The subsequent narrative shows this to mean that people from a great variety of places could hear them in their own languages as they spoke of 'the mighty works of God' (11). It is not certain whether this means that wherever a man came from he would find one or other of the speakers who used his own language or whether God rendered the words of every speaker intelligible to every hearer. Whichever be the truth there was something fantastic happening, and the crowds were amazed. Notice that the characteristic of the gift on this day was intelligibility, whereas in the gift of 'tongues' of which Paul writes later the characteristic was unintelligibility (1 Cor. 14.2). These were evidently different gifts.

Peter went on to address the crowd. He told them that they were witnessing the fulfilment of the prophecy of Joel 2.28 ff. His address both brought home the guilt of those who crucified Jesus and brought out the purpose of God (23). When people questioned him he pointed out that they too could have the gift of the Spirit. They must first repent and be baptized for the forgiveness of their sins. But then the Spirit would be given (38).

Questions and themes for study and discussion on Studies 27-31

1. What connection do you see between peace (John 14.27) and the Holy Spirit?
2. What are the implications of the gift of the Spirit for the Church's mission?

3. What should the power of the Holy Spirit mean for your life?
4. What is the significance of Acts 2.38, 39 for the modern Church?

SIX

The Spirit and the Growing Church

32 : Filled with the Spirit

Acts 4

The gift of the Spirit on the day of Pentecost did not mean that on that one day alone the Church enjoyed the divine enablement. Throughout the Acts of the Apostles we keep reading of the work of the Spirit. To such an extent is this the case that it has been seriously suggested that a better title for that book would be 'The Acts of the Holy Spirit'. It is what the Spirit is doing that is important. He works through human instruments indeed, but it is the Holy Spirit who does the significant work, not the instruments.

We see an example of this when Peter and John were arrested for their preaching of the resurrection (2 f.). Jesus had promised that in such situations His followers would be given the help of the Holy Spirit to show them what to say (Luke 12.11 f.). And so it proved. When the authorities inquired of them. Peter was 'filled with the Holy Spirit' (8) and spoke boldly It is important to see that he did not glorify the Spirit but Jesus. And when the authorities heard and saw the apostles 'they recognized that they had been with Jesus' (13). The Spirit never draws attention to Himself. He glorifies Christ (John 16.13 f.).

The release of the apostles led to a prayer meeting of their friends. The praying group recalled Scripture that applied to the circumstances and saw in the fact further evidence of the working of the Spirit. They did not see David himself as responsible for the words, but God, for they prayed 'Sovereign Lord . . . who by the mouth of our father David, thy servant, didst say by the Holy Spirit . . .' (24 f.). The Holy Spirit inspired the words that met their need.

At the conclusion of their prayer the place where they were was shaken, which we should take as a manifestation of divine power. And they were all filled with the Holy Spirit. Once again they were equipped for the service they should render and the result was that they 'spoke the word of God with boldness' (31).

Throughout the chapter we see the Spirit of God at work, directing the people of God and enabling them to render the service they should.

33 : The Serving of Tables
Acts 6.1–10; 11.19–24

There was a little quarrelling among the early Christians as to who was getting the better of the deal in 'the daily distribution' (**6**.1). The dispute concerned the serving of tables (**6**.2), a task which the apostles did not think they should discharge themselves. But they did not regard it as of little importance on that account. It mattered, and it mattered who did it. So, for this work of serving tables, they urged the rest of the believers to choose seven men 'of good repute, full of the Spirit and of wisdom' (**6**.3). We should think hard about the implications of these qualifications. We are apt to think that a man needs the Spirit for any work of preaching and teaching. But we do not give the presence of the Spirit the same emphasis when it is a matter of administration, much less of waiting at tables. The apostles saw that there are many gifts of the Spirit and that a man needs some gift for any task in the church. So the men to serve at tables were to be full of the Spirit.

We must presume that this direction was carried out, though the presence of the Spirit is mentioned only in the case of Stephen (**6**.5). Now we notice a further point of importance. These men had been chosen for the lowly service of serving at tables and for that they needed the Spirit. But serving thus in the power of the Spirit they were able to do other things also. Presently we find Stephen doing 'great wonders and signs' (**6**.8). And when he disputed with opponents 'they could not withstand the wisdom and the Spirit with which he spoke' (**6**.10). So does the presence of the Spirit manifest itself.

In due course this Spirit-filled man was arrested and martyred, and a persecution of Christians was initiated. This caused a scattering of believers which affected the work of another Spirit-filled man, Barnabas (**11**.24). From the lowly beginning in serving at tables the Spirit led Stephen on to fuller service, and even after his death the work he began went on. The same Spirit filled men like Barnabas to enable them to do the work to which they were called.

34 : The Spirit and the Samaritans

Acts 8.1–24

The spread of the gospel to Samaria meant that, for the first time, people outside the Jewish community became Christians. The fact that Philip baptized them and that subsequently Peter and John were sent to them by the apostles at Jerusalem (14) is probably connected with this new situation. With centuries of Church history behind us it never occurs to us that Christianity could be anything other than a faith for men of every nation. But in those first days many must have remembered that Jesus worked almost entirely among the Jews (Matt. **15**.24), that He sent the Twelve only to the lost sheep of the house of Israel and that the Samaritans were specifically excluded from the scope of the mission (Matt. **10**.5 f.). Jesus' teaching was probably understood at first mostly along the lines of a reforming Judaism and some of the more conservative souls in the early Church would have been hesitant about welcoming Samaritan believers, particularly in view of the normal Jewish attitude to Samaritans. It was important that it be shown on the highest level that the entry of these Samaritans into the Church was welcome. So the two chief apostles were sent to give public testimony to this effect.

When Peter and John laid hands on the new believers they received the Holy Spirit (17). The Spirit comes on all God's people. There is no specially favoured race or specially favoured group. Samaritans as well as Jews received the Spirit and in due course Gentiles as well. There are difficulties connected with the delay in the gift until the apostles came. More usually the Spirit is associated with the very beginnings (e.g. Acts 2.38). Perhaps the delay is connected with the importance of making it clear at the highest level that the Samaritans were wanted. But Scripture does not tell us and we are left to conjecture.

The other point that we must notice is that the Spirit is God's gift. Simon thought he could buy the power to confer the Spirit (18 f.). But he was quite wrong. His request showed that he had 'neither part nor lot in this matter' (21). No man can control the Spirit, either to give or to withhold the gift. The Spirit is not constrained within ecclesiastical or sacramental channels. God gives the gift. All that is left for men is to receive it and to profit by it.

35 : The Spirit and the Gentiles

Acts 10.44–11.18

The story moves on. First the Spirit was given to the Jews, then to the Samaritans. Now we read of His coming to the Gentiles, people who by no stretch of the imagination could be brought within the scope of the ancient people of God. In response to God's command and under the leading of the Spirit (11.12) Peter went to tell Cornelius and the people gathered in his house the things God had told him to say (10.33). When he did so 'the Holy Spirit fell on all who heard the word' (10.44). Peter immediately recognized this as just what had happened to Jewish believers (10.47) and later, when he defended his action against the criticisms of the circumcision party, he said that the Spirit fell on these Gentiles 'just as on us at the beginning' (11.15). That there was no difference between the gift made to the Jewish believers at first and to the Gentiles now is given emphasis. Pentecost had marked the gift of the Spirit to the Church at large, Samaria had shown that this was not a narrowly particularistic gift for Jews only, and now the happening in the house of Cornelius completed the process by showing that God gave His Spirit to Gentiles just as freely and just as fully as He did to the Jews.

This was a revolutionary thought for first century Jews, and it is not in the slightest surprising that some of the believers should have taken issue with Peter. Typically they fastened on the matter of table fellowship (11.3). Jews were very particular about food laws, for they saw it as very easy to contract defilement by eating food contaminated by some Gentile practice. Peter defended himself, first, by relating the vision in which God had spoken to him about the impossibility of calling common anything that God had pronounced clean and, secondly, by telling how the Spirit fell on the new converts in Cornelius' house. He saw in this the fulfilment of Jesus' prophecy, 'you shall be baptized with the Holy Spirit' (11.16). His question, 'who was I that I could withstand God?' (11.17) was unanswerable and it silenced his opponents. But when they regained their speech they praised God and recognized that it was His will that life should be given to the Gentiles (11.18). They may have been slow to change their ways, but their minds were not closed. They could respond to a new initiative of the Spirit.

36 : The Spirit and the Missionaries

Acts 13.1–12

We are so familiar with the concept of missionary work that we scarcely pause to think what an unusual phenomenon it is. People have always been ready, of course, to convert others to their particular point of view. But it is not common to find men giving themselves over entirely to this sort of thing. It does not come naturally to men to go out with the gospel. Our passage makes it clear that initially they did so only because the Spirit led them into it.

First, He commanded the church at Antioch, 'Set apart for me Barnabas and Saul for the work to which I have called them' (2). What this work was to be the Spirit apparently did not say. And Luke does not record for us how the church came to hear the voice of the Spirit. All that we know is that the Christians were worshipping and fasting and that somehow the Spirit conveyed His meaning to them. And the believers obeyed. They fasted and prayed, which marked what they were doing as especially significant. Then they laid their hands on the apostles and sent them off. In a way it was the church that sent them away (3). But in another way it was the Holy Spirit (4). He willed that these men should go off on a missionary journey and they went. But this does not mean that the church played a merely passive part in the proceedings. The believers certainly worshipped and fasted and prayed, and we may fairly conclude that they also gave some hard thought to the situation. And as they left themselves open to the Spirit's leading they were led in the way in which they should go.

Luke does not say that the whole voyage was carried out in the strength and under the leadership of the Spirit but he implies that this was so. He tells us that, when the apostles were opposed by Elymas, Paul took action. But only as and because he was 'filled with the Holy Spirit' (9). We should surely conclude that this momentous venture was begun, and carried through, by men under the continuing leadership of the Spirit of God.

37 : The Spirit and the Baptism of John

Acts 18.24–19.7

Apollos was clearly an outstanding man, eloquent and learned. He had acquired some knowledge of 'the way of the Lord' before he comes before us, and this possibly refers to instruction received in his native Alexandria. We should probably take 'fervent in spirit' (**18**.25) to refer to his human spirit (even though in Rom. **12**.11 a similar expression is understood by the RSV of the Holy Spirit). In this case there is no explicit reference to his being given the gift of the Spirit. Perhaps, as Lampe and others think, he had a special commission from the Lord and the Spirit was given to him then. In view of the following incident at Ephesus it is curious that there is no mention of Apollos being baptized in the name of Jesus. But we know so little about what the first Christians thought about baptism that we cannot be dogmatic in this area.

The people Paul found at Ephesus were called 'disciples' (**19**.1), which apparently means that they saw themselves as Christians, even though they had been baptized only with John's baptism. The significant thing about this incident is the first question Paul asked, 'Did you receive the Holy Spirit when you believed?' (**19**.2). It is not the question that would spontaneously arise from most modern Christians in a similar situation. It shows the centrality of the Spirit for Paul. If a man was a Christian then he would have the Spirit.

Paul found that they had known only John's baptism, so they were now baptized in the name of Jesus. The apostle then laid his hands on them and they received the Spirit, spoke with tongues, and prophesied (**19**.6). This is the third mention of this kind of laying on of hands in Acts (see **8**.17; **9**.17). No reason is given for this action in these cases only. That it was not a necessity is shown by the gift of the Spirit on occasions when it was not used (e.g. **10**.44). But it is a suitable gesture to convey thoughts like fellowship and blessing. Sometimes, as here, those who received the Spirit spoke with tongues. There is no indication why this should take place on some occasions and not others. But the important thing is the presence of the Spirit, not our inability to explain other issues.

Questions and themes for study and discussion on Studies 32-37

1. What do we learn from Acts 4 about the resources open to the Christian and the way they should be used?
2. For what tasks in the modern Church should we seek the help of the Spirit?
3. What significance do you see in the coming of the Spirit to despised Samaritans?
4. What conclusions should we draw for our own work from the Spirit's actions in Acts 13?
5. How central is the Holy Spirit in your way of life?

SEVEN

The Spirit and the Christian Life

38 : The Spirit and the Law
Galatians 3.1–14

The great question which every religion must ultimately face is 'law or grace?' For Christians there can be no doubt about the answer. The cross is absolutely central; in the literal sense of the word it is 'crucial'. And that means that our salvation is all of grace. It is God's good gift, not something that we earn by our good lives, our prayers, our devotional or liturgical habits, or by anything else whatever. Our salvation was costly: Christ became 'a curse for us' (13). But it is complete. We are now redeemed from the law's curse (13).

Some of the Galatians had evidently overlooked this. There are difficulties in interpreting parts of this letter, for Paul does not explain in detail what the trouble was, and we are left to fill in some of the gaps. But there seems little doubt that the Galatians were first converted as they heard salvation by grace preached powerfully, and that afterwards some of them were persuaded that the path to fuller progress in the faith lay in keeping the law, as Judaism prescribed. Paul's response is to point out that this violates the central teaching of Christianity.

He assumes that the presence of the Spirit in the lives of believers is basic. He does not argue for it, but asks how the Galatians got it—was it 'by works of the law, or by hearing with faith' (2)? That the Spirit is God's gift and not the result of any process by which the Christian piles up merit is a fundamental proposition. If we had to earn the Spirit's presence, then the whole character of Christianity would be changed. Paul is emphasizing that God is interested, not only in forgiving our sins, but also in being with us, guiding us and strengthening us so that we may live lives of fruitful service. So He puts His Spirit within the hearts of all His people. Again there is the thought that the Spirit is not the preserve of a few outstanding souls. Paul adds the thought that God's gift is not something on which we can improve. We begin our Christian lives 'with the Spirit'. It is folly to think we can go on 'with the flesh' (3). God does miracles in believers. But He does them by His Spirit in response to faith, not 'law works' (5). We cannot emphasize too strongly the importance of seeing the Spirit's presence in our hearts as God's gift. Take that away and what is left is not Christianity.

39 : The Spirit and the Flesh

Galatians 5.13–6.10

It is important that the Christian life is lived in freedom. The believer is not tied down with burdensome restrictions as he lives out the freedom that Christ bestows (John 8.34 ff.). But where there is liberty there is always the temptation to licence, the temptation to use liberty 'as an opportunity for the flesh', i.e. for the lower nature (5.13). There is always a conflict between 'the desires of the flesh' and 'the desires of the Spirit' (5.17). We should not think of 'the flesh' as no more than crude lust. It can be that, but it can also be a highly cultured self-centredness. It is anything which means concentration on the self and the self's concerns without regard to the good of others or the will of God. The dreadful list in 5.19–21 shows what this can lead to.

But when the Spirit of God comes into a man's life there is a new power which enables him to overcome self-centredness. This is not by pointing him to a list of laws (5.18). He lives in freedom. But in this freedom qualities are developed like love (which significantly heads the list), joy, peace and the rest (5.22 f.). These qualities are not provided by the Christian's trying hard. They are 'fruit', the natural result of the Spirit's indwelling.

This does not mean that the believer does nothing but sit back and wait for the Spirit's fruit to appear. There is nothing in our passage to justify spiritual laziness. The believer is commanded (this word is not too strong and must be borne in mind even in the midst of our freedom), 'walk by the Spirit' (5.16). He is to walk (i.e. his behaviour is to be controlled) by the Spirit as well as live by the Spirit (5.25). He is to sow to the Spirit (6.8)—perhaps placing the emphasis on future planning. He is to crucify the flesh (5.24) and refuse to gratify its desires (5.16). And throughout our passage Paul has scattered a number of injunctions to positive and negative deeds incumbent on the believer. There is something paradoxical about all this. But the believer finds in his experience that both sides of the paradox are true. He must wage a constant war against the flesh, for if he gives in to it the works of the flesh become manifest in his life. But when he determinedly sets himself against the flesh and looks to the Spirit for the strength he needs, the fruit of the Spirit is his. He does not earn it. It is God's gift. But he does not get it if he opts for the self-centred life.

40 : The Law of the Spirit of Life

Romans 8.1–27

In this classic discussion of life in the Spirit Paul draws an emphatic contrast between life 'according to the flesh' and life 'according to the Spirit' (4 f.). The 'flesh' will mean the lower nature and living 'according to the flesh', the self-centred life. Paul emphasizes the 'set' of the life (5) and points out that it is 'death' to set one's mind on the flesh (6). Notice that he does not say it will bring death but that it is death. To reject the Holy Spirit of God and to live one's self-centred life on the basis of private interests and concerns is death here and now. The man who chooses to 'live' in this way by that very fact cuts himself off from all that life 'in the Spirit' means. He sentences himself to a petty, meagre little existence, instead of 'the glorious liberty of the children of God' (21).

A second point emphasized here is the presence of the Spirit in the life of the believer. All Christians have the Spirit. Paul puts this both negatively (9) and positively (14). This sharply differentiates Christianity from the other religions of antiquity. They knew of spirit-inspired men, but they were few in number and regarded as specially favoured. It was something quite new when the Christians taught that every believer had the Spirit.

The third thing our passage emphasizes is the freedom that is characteristic of Christians. Those in whom the Spirit dwells have received no 'spirit of slavery' (15). Bondage is the very antithesis of the Christian way, for believers enjoy 'the spirit of sonship'. Now sonship in the heavenly family means being heirs together with Christ (17) and this means freedom (21). The creation as such does not know this kind of freedom. Creation is subject to futility (20) and for men who are part of creation, this means suffering (18). But for the Christian all this futility is transformed. The presence of the Spirit means that life has meaning. Even suffering fits into the pattern. The sufferings of Christ were meaningful and brought salvation to believers. The sufferings of believers have their meaning too and they are to be seen as no more than incidents on the way to the realization of the Christian hope.

Finally, Paul tells us that the Spirit helps us in our praying (26). Our prayers at best are tepid and feeble. But the Spirit Himself assists us and intercedes for us.

41 : The Gifts of the Spirit

1 Corinthians 12

It was accepted among the religions of the first century that from time to time a 'divine' spirit would come upon men. His presence would be shown by unusual behaviour, probably of an ecstatic type. Clearly the Corinthian Christians were influenced by this view and they thought that the more spectacular manifestations were, of necessity, evidence of the Spirit's presence among them. It is probably this that lies behind Paul's words about saying 'Jesus be cursed!' (3). Someone had, perhaps, uttered some garbled expression of the thought that Christ became a 'curse' for us (Gal. 3.13), and the Corinthians, impressed by the excitement with which the words were uttered, imagined they showed possession by the Spirit. Paul denies this and goes on to the thought that only by the Spirit can one really acknowledge Jesus as Lord. Anyone can, of course, say the words, but only the Spirit-enlightened man can mean them. It is the content of a man's words, not the excitement with which he utters them, that shows the presence of the Spirit. The Spirit witnesses to Jesus (John 15.26).

Paul proceeds to the thought that the Spirit gives a variety of good gifts to God's people. Nobody is left out, for to each the Spirit gives some gift for the common good (7). The gifts of the Spirit are to build up the church, not simply to please the recipients. Paul lists a number of such gifts (8 ff.). Some of them are rather puzzling and commentators find it difficult, for example, to put a clear distinction between 'the utterance of wisdom' and 'the utterance of knowledge' and between the 'through' which applies to the former and the 'according to' used of the latter (8).

There are problems also with regard to the gift of faith (9), for as all Christians have faith, this must be a special gift. There are problems also with healings (why the plural in the Greek?) and with others. We find problems also with the gifts listed at the end of the chapter (28 ff.) though without the mention of the Spirit. It is probably best not to try to work out what it was exactly that God gave the early Church, but rather to concentrate on using to the full the gifts that He gives His people today. In some cases they will be the same, but they may well differ. We should 'earnestly desire' the gifts that are best for our day (31).

42 : Love is the Greatest

1 Corinthians 13

The Holy Spirit is not mentioned in specific terms in this chapter. But it would be a mistake to think that He is not in mind. In chs. 12–14 Paul is engaged in a sustained argument about the 'gifts' of the Spirit. It is plain that the Corinthians were impressed by the more spectacular gifts, like speaking in tongues, and the discussion in ch. 12 shows that there had been some jealousies and hard feelings. Paul does not disparage the gifts the Corinthians prized. He recognizes that such gifts come from God and he thinks that all who have received them should use them. But he is just as clear that it is not these gifts that matter most. When he wrote to the Galatians he listed the 'fruit' of the Spirit and began with love (Gal. 5.22). So now he takes time to emphasize that the 'more excellent way' (12.31) is the way of love.

We should not understand the love of which he writes as a merely human achievement. John can say, 'In this is love, not that we loved God . . .' (1 John 4.10). If we start from the human end we shall never understand the distinctive Christian idea of love. It is God's love that gives us the clue. John goes on, 'but that he loved us and sent his Son to be the expiation (better, "propitiation") for our sins.' It is the divine love shown in the cross, where the sinless Jesus died for sinners, that shows us what love is. When a man sees this and responds to it a change takes place. He is transformed by the power of the Holy Spirit and begins to see men in a measure as God sees them, as people for whom Christ died. He cannot accordingly regard them as indifferent. They are the objects of God's love and now of his also.

The Spirit brings it about that the Christian comes to love the unworthy, love them for what God has done in him and them and not for their inherent qualities. 1 Cor. 13 spells out in some detail what this means in terms of daily living. The Spirit-filled man is mindful of what he can do for others rather than what he can get for himself. Love is the mainspring of his action.

43 : Speaking in 'Tongues'

1 Corinthians 14

One of the gifts of the Spirit which the Corinthians clearly prized was that of speaking in 'tongues'. This was apparently the uttering of sounds that neither the speaker nor any of his hearers understood unless they had the gift of interpretation. The characteristic was thus its unintelligibility (2). It denoted an activity of the spirit of the man, but not of his mind (14). It was more spectacular than love and the like, and it is not surprising that the volatile Corinthians valued it highly.

Paul is clear that this kind of speech really is a gift from the Spirit (2), and he refuses to forbid its use (39). But because of its unintelligibility he does not regard it as being as important as say, prophecy, an activity in which the hearers are edified. So he prefers prophecy to speaking in 'tongues' (5). His guiding principle is 'all things should be done decently and in order' (40). It is important that the church be edified and thus he strongly prefers the intelligible gifts. From the little glimpse he gives us of the church at worship (26 ff.) it is clear that there was a good deal of spontaneity. But it is clear, too, that what mattered most of all was edification.

A question of some importance is whether the gift of 'tongues' should be exercised in modern times. Those in the 'charismatic' movement hold that it should. Those outside it often hold that it should not. In favour of the former view is the fact that the New Testament nowhere says it should cease. In favour of the latter, the New Testament nowhere says it should continue, and in fact it does not seem to have continued. Quite early in the Church's history 'tongues' and some other gifts appear to have ceased. It is quite possible to hold that they were meant for the time of the Church's infancy. At the present time what is surely needed is charitable tolerance. If 'tongues' is a continuing gift and God grants it to a believer, he must use it. But he must not belittle another who does not have it. Similarly, he who has had no such experience would do well not to scorn him who claims it. Finally, it should be noted that there is no scriptural warrant for holding that the presence of any particular gift, be it 'tongues' or any other, is, in itself, evidence of the special presence of the Spirit.

44 : The Seal and the Pledge

2 Corinthians 1.21, 22; 5.1–5; Ephesians 1.11–14

When many were illiterate it was of little use to write one's name on anything to denote possession. But a seal with a characteristic pattern was another matter. The most illiterate and unlearned could recognize that. So when it was important that people in general should know whose an article was, the imprint of a seal would be put on it. The seal thus was a mark of ownership. When the Spirit is regarded as the seal (2 Cor. 1.22; Eph. 1.13) the thought is that it is the presence of the Spirit that shows that a man belongs to Christ. Without the Spirit we are not His (Rom. 8.9). It is in line with this that when Paul met some men who claimed to be disciples he immediately asked them, 'Did you receive the Holy Spirit when you believed?' (Acts 19.2). That is the decisive question.

In all three of our passages the Spirit is also called a 'guarantee' (2 Cor. 1.22; 5.5; Eph. 1.14). This picturesque word is used for the down payment in a variety of transactions. Moulton and Milligan cite a lady, selling a cow, who received 1,000 drachmas as down payment. They speak also of a mouse-catcher who received 8 drachmas (the rest presumably when he caught the mice!), and of some dancing girls in whose case it is specifically laid down that the earnest money was part of the full price. In each case the money is a first instalment. It is a guarantee that the remainder will come in due course. In modern Greek this term has come to mean an engagement ring, an excellent illustration of the force of the word. It is something now, but it looks for better things to come.

So with the Holy Spirit. The Spirit's presence is a priceless gift here and now. But, wonderful though it is, this is no more than a beginning. That God gives us the Spirit shows that He means business. And He will certainly complete what He has begun. The believer can look forward to the life to come knowing that it will be more richly blessed than this present one.

45 : The Spirit and Wisdom
Ephesians 1.15–23; 3.14–21

It is uncertain whether the word 'spirit' in 1.17 should be spelled with a small 's' as in the RSV (in which case the reference is to the man's inner life) or a capital (in which case the Holy Spirit is meant). There seems no way of deciding the point and exegetes will probably continue to differ. But in practice it does not make a great deal of difference. Paul is not speaking of a natural endowment, but of what the Holy Spirit does in believers. Even if we understand the text to mean 'the spiritual powers of wisdom and vision' (NEB), we must take this as referring to the Spirit's good gifts. True wisdom and that revelation that brings the knowledge of God come from the Holy Spirit. They are not the product of human achievement. This does not mean that every Christian is wiser than every non-Christian. But it does mean that every Christian who gives heed to the leadings of the Spirit is a much wiser man than he was before he became a Christian. So is it with vision. The Spirit-filled man has his vision constantly enlarged. And as his horizon extends so he grows in his knowledge of God.

Our second passage brings us a kindred thought, though this time it is more the idea of strength than of insight that is stressed. It is not easy to live the Christian life in a world like ours. If we are to do this we need a strength not our own. It is an important characteristic of the Christian way that it does not simply tell a man how to live and leave it at that. It equips him for living. Paul is fond of contrasting mere words with power (cf. 1 Cor. 1.17; 2.4) and, while the contrast is not explicit here, the power is real. The Spirit strengthens a believer 'with might . . . in the inner man' (3.16). The man in whom the Spirit lives is stronger by far than he ever was before he received the gift. And this leads on to the indwelling of Christ and to that 'being rooted and grounded in love' that leads ultimately to 'all the fullness of God' (3.17–19). It is only as the Spirit is within us that we have this gift.

46 : Exhilaration in the Spirit

Ephesians 5.15–21; 6.10–20

The contrast between getting 'drunk with wine' and being filled 'with the Spirit' (5.18) is noteworthy, especially in view of the staid and solemn demeanour that characterizes so much of modern Christianity. Clearly, to the early Christians the presence of the Spirit was an exhilarating affair and life in the Spirit far from sedate. On the day of Pentecost believers had been accused of being drunk (Acts 2.13, 15) and it is interesting to see Paul anticipating that believers who have God's Spirit will manifest conduct comparable to that of the inebriated.

It is not certain that 'be filled with the Spirit' is the right translation, for the construction is unusual to say the least. Abbott maintains that it is never used in the sense 'be filled with' (I.C.C.). It is rather 'be filled in', i.e. 'be filled in (your) spirit'. This would mean that the believer is to have his fullness in the higher part of his nature, not the lower. But, as this would take place only through the work of the Spirit, in the end it comes to much the same.

When he comes to the 'whole armour of God' Paul twice finds a place for what the Spirit does. He speaks of 'the sword of the Spirit' (which he explains as 'the word of God') and again of prayer 'in the Spirit' (6.17 f.). We should not overlook the fact that the sword is an attacking weapon. Much of the armour of which Paul writes is defensive and shields us from the attacks of the evil one. But when the Christian goes on the offensive he does so with the aid of the Word of God. It is this that enables him to advance. We must know our Bibles and know how to handle them if we are to see progress in the faith. With this we must take prayer in the Spirit. We usually see prayer as a human activity and, of course, in part it is. But it is the Spirit who enables us to pray effectually (cf. Rom. 8.26 f.). As we pray it is important to look for the Spirit's guidance and enabling. If we see it as a purely human activity we shall surely lack power in our prayer.

47 : All have Knowledge

1 John 2.18–27; 3.23, 24

In the first century there appear to have been some religious systems that stressed the importance of a knowledge firmly in the hands of a religious élite. Holding 'the key of knowledge', so to speak, the possessors were able to let people in by giving them the right instruction (and, of course, to keep them out if they withheld it!). Only those so initiated could be saved. Christianity came out in radical opposition to all such systems and John insists on this when he says, 'you have been anointed by the Holy One, and you all know' (2.20). The language is unusual, but the meaning is not in doubt. The Holy One is the Being usually called the Holy Spirit and His coming on people is the 'anointing'. When, then, the Spirit comes upon people they have knowledge. They all have it. This does not mean that there is no room for instruction in the Christian faith or for believers going on from a less perfect to a more perfect understanding of the faith. The very existence of the New Testament in itself shows this to be wrong. Every book of the New Testament is written to bring men knowledge, and there are many reminders of the importance of studying the things of God. No, there is much room for all of us to grow in knowledge of the Bible and of the God to whom it points, and we can help one another to do so. What John is saying is that this knowledge is open to every Christian. In principle there is no piece of Christian knowledge which is not open to the apprehension of the humblest believer.

This anointing, John further says, 'abides in you' (2.27). The Spirit remains and continues to enlighten God's people. In this respect they have no need of any teacher. One Christian may help another, but in the last resort advance in the Christian way depends on heeding the indwelling Spirit. There is no substitute for the teaching He gives. It is imperative that we be constantly alert for His voice and that we heed what we hear. It is this constant experience of the presence of the Spirit that gives us assurance (3.24). There is nothing outward and visible that shows that God is in us. But that does not mean we are left in doubt and uncertainty. Day by day we have experience of the Holy Spirit and His leading, and it is by this that we know God is in us.

Questions and themes for study and discussion on Studies 38-47

1. What do you understand by 'the glorious liberty of the children of God'?
2. What 'gifts' do you see the Spirit as giving to the Church today?
3. How far are you showing love in your daily living?
4. How can your gifts be used to edify the church?
5. What does 2 Cor. 5.1–4 tell us of the inheritance of which the Holy Spirit is our guarantee?
6. How may the believer be sure of growing in wisdom and in vision and in power?
7. How are you using 'the sword of the Spirit' for advance?
8. What has the Holy Spirit taught you today?

EIGHT

The Spirit and the Holy Scriptures

48 : God has Spoken
2 Samuel 23.1–7; Mark 12.35–37

One of the great thoughts of the Old Testament is that God has spoken to men. Expressions abound like 'Thus says the Lord . . .', or 'The word of the Lord came to . . .' It has been calculated that such turns of speech occur more than 3,000 times. Often they introduce quite long sections. So here David says, 'The Spirit of the Lord speaks by me' (2 Sam. 23.2). The Spirit is using David as His means of communication. That is to say, David's words are more than a merely human utterance. This does not mean that they are not a human utterance. They are. Every passage in scripture bears the hallmarks of its human authorship. David does not write like Jeremiah, Paul like John. Each writer uses his own method and style. Each employs his own range of knowledge and skills. Each says what seems to be indicated by the situation in which he finds himself. The individuality of the inspired writers is plain and important.

But that is not the whole story. David insists on two things: God spoke to him and God spoke through him. This does not necessarily mean that David was the recipient of a sudden celestial communication. It means that God made use of David's whole personality to convey His message to men. God was with David in all his formative years and in all the years of his public life. He was with His servant in all the experiences grave and gay that went to make him the man he was. He was with him when he came to write his last words. What David wrote was in one sense the natural response of the man, being what he was, to the situation in which he found himself. In another sense it was the word of God, the word that God wanted written at that time. This is emphasized by the fourfold repetition in 2 Sam. 23.2 f. What David was writing was God's word.

And that is what Jesus said about it, too. He maintained that David was 'inspired by the Holy Spirit' (Mark 12.36) when he wrote Psa. 110. The Greek might be rendered 'David said in the

Holy Spirit' which comes to much the same. Either way Jesus is saying that the Spirit worked in God's servant in such a way that what was written was what God wanted written.

49 : 'God-breathed'

2 Timothy 3.10–17

Timothy came from a believing family (2 Tim. 1.5) and he had had the benefit of a godly upbringing. This meant that he had received a thorough grounding in 'the sacred writings' (15), i.e. the scriptures of the Old Testament. Notice that these 'are able to instruct you for salvation through faith in Christ Jesus' (15). The way of salvation may be clearer in the New Testament than in the Old, but we must never forget that the Old is sacred scripture too, and that it points to Christ.

Paul goes on to say, 'All scripture is inspired by God' (16). His word is *theopneustos*, found only here in the New Testament and not very often outside it. B. B. Warfield conducted a monumental examination of this word as a result of which he showed that it must be understood in the sense 'breathed of God'. That is to say its use marks scripture as the utterance of God. It is not that the Scriptures were produced and that then God somehow breathed into (in-spired) them. They were produced by God's breathing them, i.e. speaking them. Nothing could be said surely that affirms more strongly the reliability of scripture. God spoke the words of scripture. He spoke them, certainly, through the prophets and others, but He spoke them. It is this that causes Paul to accord such a high place to scripture.

Some translations have renderings like, 'Every scripture inspired of God is also profitable . . .' (RV). This has led to the view that some scripture is inspired and some is not, which opens the way for the rejection of what we find unpalatable. But against this, in the first place the AV (KJV), ARV and RSV translate correctly, and in the second, it does not matter greatly if we do accept the RV, for it is impossible to hold that Paul is differentiating between inspired and uninspired scripture. Nothing in any of his writings leads us to think that such a distinction was possible for him. He saw the whole of scripture as God's utterance and, however we translate, that is what he is saying here.

50 : Scripture's Origin

2 Peter 1.16–2.3; 1 John 4.1–6

The whole of our first passage stresses the reliability of Scripture in contrast to the 'cleverly devised myths' (2 Pet. 1.16) of 'false prophets' and 'false teachers' (2.1). In every century some have preferred their own ideas to those revealed in the Bible. Against this Peter insists on its divine origin. 'No prophecy of scripture,' he says, 'is a matter of one's own interpretation' (1.20). But *epiluseos*, translated 'interpretation', means basically an unloosing, an untying. The context (as well as the word's proper meaning) is against the thought of 'interpretation' and strongly favours that of 'origin'. Peter is saying that scriptural prophecy did not take its point of release from men, or perhaps was not the result of men's unravelling of problems. He is not speaking about the way the Bible should be interpreted but the way it arose. This is reinforced when he goes on to say that the originating force was not 'the impulse of man'. Rather 'men moved by the Holy Spirit spoke from God' (1.21). His word 'moved' (*pheromenoi*) means 'carried along'. Peter is not denying the human element in prophecy. But he is denying that the human element is all there is. He is saying that the Holy Spirit carried the inspired writers where they should go. Michael Green points out that the same verb is used of a ship carried along with the wind (Acts 27.15, 17) and comments: 'The prophets raised their sails, so to speak (they were obedient and receptive), and the Holy Spirit filled them and carried their craft along in the direction He wished.'

Where Peter speaks of the origin John refers to the result. It must have been a problem for members of the early Church to know who among all those claiming to give authentic teaching about God were to be believed (as it still is). John says the test is the teaching about Jesus. The Spirit of God is known when men give clear witness to the incarnation (1 John 4.2), that is to say, when they see Jesus as the Christ, God's divine Messiah, 'come in the flesh' (really human). Where the emphasis is on anything else we are in the presence of the spirit of error, not of truth (1 John 4.6). The attitude to Jesus is the touchstone.

97 The Spirit and the Tabernacle

Hebrews 9.1–10; 10.11–18

Modern Christians often find little to grip them in the detailed regulations of Leviticus. They see this book as full of liturgical minutiae, completely irrelevant for people who must live in our quite different circumstances and for whom that whole way of religion is history. Not so the writer of the Epistle to the Hebrews. For him the tabernacle belonged to a bygone age indeed (though, of course, the Temple retained many of the same features). But that was not the important thing. What mattered was that the ancient tabernacle had been set up under divine direction. The Holy Spirit of God had caused writers of old time to set down regulations for its construction and use. So he speaks of the arrangements whereby in the outer 'tent' were objects like the lampstand and the table (9.2) and in the inner one, the Holy of Holies, other objects, notably the ark of the covenant and the mercy seat (9.3–5). From that he goes on to refer to the ministry of the priests and specifically to that of the high priest on the Day of Atonement. In the fact that the High Priest alone entered the Holy of Holies, and he only on that one day in the year, our author sees the Holy Spirit as teaching men. The Spirit is showing (by the limited access granted under the old covenant) that the way into the very presence of God was not yet open (9.8). The Spirit speaks through what He has caused men to record of the old way.

The Spirit speaks also through what is recorded about the new covenant. Our author is particularly interested in the forgiveness of sins, which, he sees, could not be brought about by the Levitical sacrifices (10.11). He sets Christ's sacrifice of Himself in sharp contrast to them. Its utter finality is attested by no less than the Holy Spirit Himself, for it was the Spirit who spoke through the prophet Jeremiah when he linked the forgiveness of sins with the new covenant. Thus in both the ritual of the old covenant, and in the prophecy of its supersession by the new covenant, we have evidence of God's ways given us by the Holy Spirit.

Questions and themes for study and discussion on Studies 48-51

1. Reflect on the implications of 'his word is upon my tongue' (2 Sam. 23.2).

2. What difference does it make to a modern Christian that the Old Testament is 'God-breathed'?
3. Men spoke. God spoke. We must neglect neither fact.
4. '*All* scripture is inspired by God and profitable . . .' (2 Tim. 3.16). Not just those parts we personally find stimulating.